THE EARTH STRIKES BACK

HOW WE CAN SAVE OUR PLANET

AIR AND ENERGY

Arthur Haswell

Chrysalis Children's Books

First published in Great Britain in 2000 by
Chrysalis Children's Books
    An imprint of Chrysalis Books Group Plc
    The Chrysalis Building, Bramley Road, London W10 6SP

Paperback edition first published in 2004
Copyright © Chrysalis Books Group Plc 2000
Text copyright © Arthur Haswell 2000

Editor Molly Perham
Designer Helen James
Picture Researcher Kathy Lockley
Illustrator William Donohoe
Consultant Chris Baines

ISBN 1 84138 071 7 (hardback)
ISBN 1 84138 941 2 (paperback)

British Library Cataloguing in Publication Data
for this book is available from the British Library.

Printed in China

Words in **bold** are explained in the glossary
on pages 46 and 47.

Picture acknowledgements
Chris Bonington Picture Library/Doug Scott 9 B
Britstock-Ifa/Kramer 40 T
© Chrysler Jeep© Imports UK 35B
Daimler Chrysler 34
Environmental Images /Graham Burns 44, /Martin Bond 26, 28 T, 35 T, 37 B, /Michael
McKinnon 27 B, /Vanessa Miles 41
Mary Evans Picture Library 22
Geoscience Features Picture Library 24 T
Robert Harding Picture Library 16, 17 T, 17 B, 24 B, 37 T
Frank Lane Picture Agency /J C Munoz 22 T, /John Lynch 12, /John Watkins 14, /Maurice
Nimmo 7 B, /Roger Wilmshurst 13 T, /Treat Davidson 4
Panos Pictures /Clive Shirley 28 B, /Dermot Tatlow 18, /Sean Sprague 32 T
Planet Earth Pictures /Roger de la Mare 7 T, /Steve Nicholls 9 T
Rex Features 21 B, /SIPA 19 B
Science Photo Library /European Space Agency 15 B, /John Sanford 4, /Lowell Georgia 31
T, /Mark Burnett 15 T, /Martin Bond 33, /NASA 21 T, /Russel D Curtis 3, 31 T, /Simon
Fraser 13 B, 19 T, /Tommaso Guicciardini 30
Frank Spooner Pictures /Liaison 30
Still Pictures /Mike Kollofel 10, /Daniel Dancer 32 B, /Jim Olive 27 T, /Mark Edwards 20, 25
©Time News /Simon Brooke 40 B.

Contents

Air for life

Air surrounds us all the time. It is a mixture of different gases that plants and animals need to live. Air made life possible on Earth and has sustained it for around 3.5 billion years.

Our unique atmosphere

The layers of gases surrounding the Earth are the **atmosphere**. Other planets in the Solar System have gases around them, making up an atmosphere, but only the Earth has **air**. Without air, the sky would be black rather than blue, and the Sun would be a deadly ball of fire.

▲ The Moon has no atmosphere to protect it from meteors. Its surface is dotted with craters made by meteors crashing into it. The sky around the Moon is black.

Earth's shield

Every day about a million meteors reach planet Earth. These pieces of stone travel at high speed across space and crash into the surface of planets which have no atmosphere, making craters and throwing up dust. But the Earth's air acts as a shield. The meteors become so hot from the friction of falling through air that nearly all of them burn up and we see them as shooting stars. Meteorites are large rocks that do not burn up completely and hit the ground.

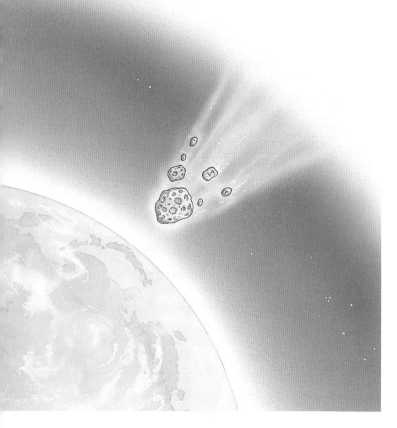

◄ Meteors crash into the Earth's atmosphere at speeds of up to 250 000 km/h. They burn up at 300 to 50 kilometres from the surface.

▲ *Air is important for insect pollination. A bee travels through the air from flower to flower, carrying pollen from the male anther of a flower on to the ripe female stigma.*

Life-giving air

Air is the most important of the natural resources that we need to sustain life. We could live without food for a few weeks, and without water for several days, but no one can survive for more than a few minutes without air.

The gases in air protect us from the Sun's harmful **radiation**, while trapping its life-giving heat. Air carries sound waves so that we can hear. It transmits smells that allow animals to communicate and mate. Insects and birds need air to fly.

Making peace with our planet

The air around us is a unique mixture of gases. Plants and animals survive by taking what they need from it. Over the last two centuries that unique mixture has been altered by human activity. We have cut down the forests that help to maintain the right mixture of gases. At the same time, factories and exhaust pipes have pumped smoke and fumes into the air and polluted it. The Earth is changing in response to what humans are doing. We need to protect our planet and make sure that air continues to support plants and animals – as well as people – in the way that it has always done.

What is air?

Air is invisible and has no taste or scent. Yet we can see the effect of air on the move, feel it against our cheeks, and smell the odours it carries.

Layers of air

The band of air around Earth extends to 700 kilometres above the surface. Within this wide band of air gases move and mix constantly. Above it, in the **exosphere**, there is very little air. The highest layer of air, directly exposed to the Sun, is called the **thermosphere**. Here temperatures can reach over 600°C. Below, in the **mesosphere**, temperatures can drop as low as -100°C. Strong winds blow in the mesosphere. The **stratosphere** underneath is dry and clouds are rare. This is where planes fly. We live in the lowest layer, the **troposphere**. Above our heads the temperature drops by 6.5°C per kilometre as you go higher. At the top of the troposphere water becomes ice.

Pulling air down

Gravity works on air just as it does on everything else on Earth – it pulls air towards the ground. Because of this, air collects and is thickest at the bottom, where we live. All the air above pushes down on each of us with the weight of almost a tonne.

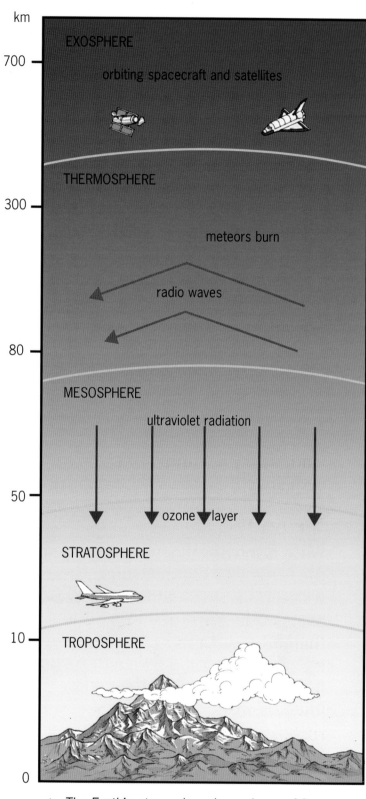

▲ *The Earth's atmosphere is made up of five main layers – the troposphere, stratosphere, mesosphere, thermosphere and exosphere. The air is thinner as you go higher, and the troposphere is the only layer in which living things can breathe normally.*

▲ *Birds of prey use pockets of warm air, called thermals, to help them stay up in the air while they circle looking for prey.*

Thinner and thinner

Air becomes thinner higher up and the pressure decreases. Beyond the troposphere air is too thin to support life. Yet the atmosphere continues, containing smaller and smaller amounts of air, until at last it merges with space.

Air on the move

Wind is moving air. The Sun produces the force that drives winds. Areas of warmer air are created when some parts of the Earth heat up more than others. As this air heats up it expands and so becomes lighter. It rises, leaving a gap – an area of low pressure – into which cooler air rushes from the sides. As air moves, it carries tiny **particles** called **aerosols** that are picked up along the way. These include pollen, salt from the sea, dust, sand and living **microbes**. Other aerosols come from sources of air **pollution**, such as chimneys and exhaust pipes.

Useful air

Some plants need the wind to carry their seeds, while others rely on insects that fly through the air for pollination. People use air in many different ways. For thousands of years boats have been equipped with sails to catch the wind and drive them along. Aeroplanes fly through the air. When we pump up a tyre we force a large amount of air into a small container to make **compressed air**. Trapped air acts as an **insulator**, so we wear several layers of clothes in the winter to keep out the cold.

Breathing air

Air is made up of different gases. The most important of these gases for life on Earth is oxygen.

All together now

Oxygen makes up about 21 per cent of the air around us. It is also found in other things, making up half the weight of rocks. Water is 89 per cent oxygen.

Almost all living things on Earth need oxygen. Only a few creatures, such as **bacteria**, can survive without it. When animals breathe, they take in oxygen from the atmosphere. It combines with food to make the energy that living cells need before they can do their work.

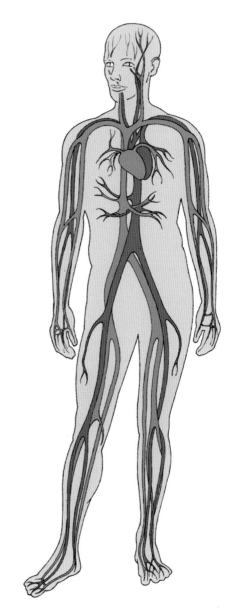

▲ The heart pumps oxygen-rich blood around the body. The waste product, carbon dioxide, returns to the lungs to be expelled.

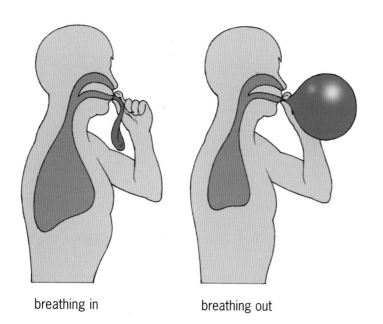

breathing in   breathing out

▲ When we breathe we take air, and any pollution in the air, directly into our bodies.

Breathe in!

Mammals, birds, amphibians and reptiles all suck air into their lungs. The air spreads through the thin lining of the lungs until it reaches the blood in tiny blood vessels. It is then loaded on to red blood cells and carried to all parts of the body. Fish have gills that allow the oxygen dissolved in water to pass into their blood. Insects draw in air through holes in their bodies.

▲ *The water beetle takes a bubble of air from the surface and holds it when it dives, so that it can breathe underwater.*

Not enough oxygen

Too little oxygen in the air can make us sleepy. In a stuffy room, where the windows are closed and lots of people are using up the oxygen and breathing out **carbon dioxide**, we start to yawn. We may feel tired or fall asleep. Opening a window is usually enough to supply the oxygen we are missing.

If someone stands still for a long time, the blood collects in their legs, and there is too little blood carrying oxygen to their brain. They may feel faint, or become unconscious. Lying down for a few minutes allows the blood supply to return to normal, and they will soon recover as the oxygen reaches their brain.

High in the atmosphere, where the air is thinner, there is not enough oxygen to keep people alive. People who climb the peaks of the world's highest mountains carry a supply of extra oxygen in metal cylinders. The pilot of a jet fighter wears a mask that covers the nose and mouth and has a pipe connected to an oxygen store within the plane. Our lungs cannot take oxygen from water, so divers strap an **aqualung** full of compressed air to their backs.

A mixture of gases

As well as oxygen, air contains a number of other gases, all mixed together. It also carries water vapour, from which clouds and rain are formed.

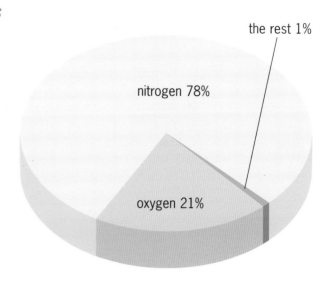

▲ *This pie chart shows the proportion of each gas in the Earth's atmosphere.*

The body builder

Nitrogen makes up 78 per cent of the air. Plants and animals need nitrogen to build their bodies. Bacteria in the soil draw nitrogen from the air. Plants take nitrogen from the soil. Animals get nitrogen by eating plants or other animals. When plants and animals die, they rot and return nitrogen to the soil. This continuous exchange of nitrogen is called the nitrogen cycle.

Photosynthesis

Plants take in carbon dioxide through their leaves and, using water and the Sun's energy, make their own food in a process called **photosynthesis**. The ability of plants to produce their own food is the basis of life on Earth.

▼ *Carbon circulates between the atmosphere and living things in the carbon cycle.*

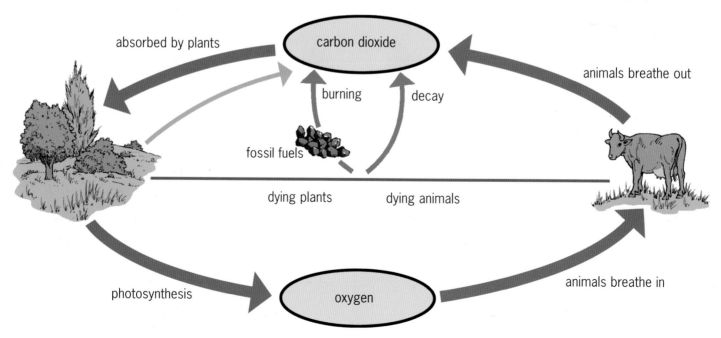

▲ *These dark clouds blowing in from the sea herald a tropical storm in the Caribbean.*

The carbon cycle

Carbon circulates through the air, plants, animals and the soil in an endless cycle. Plants draw carbon dioxide from the air; animals take in carbon when they eat plants. Animals release carbon dioxide when they breathe out, and again when they die and decompose. Forests absorb some of this carbon and release carbon dioxide into the air when they burn. In the oceans, carbon dissolves in the water and carbon dioxide is released when the water warms up.

Noble gases

Air contains small amounts of other gases. The most plentiful of these are **argon** and **neon**, both used in light bulbs and fluorescent tubes. **Helium** occurs in small amounts and weighs

Wet air

Water is taken into the air by the process of **evaporation**. It is drawn from the surface of oceans, lakes and rivers and carried in the air as **water vapour**. The amount of water vapour in the air is known as **humidity**. Desert air may have almost no water vapour, while in a rainforest the air may be 3 per cent water vapour. When air rises, it cools, and water vapour **condenses** into clouds of tiny droplets or ice crystals. When these become heavy they fall as rain or snow.

less than other gases. It is pumped into balloons and airships to make them float in the air. **Xenon** and **krypton** exist in even tinier amounts, about one part in a million. They are also used in fluorescent lights. These gases do not mix with other gases. They are called **noble gases**.

Changing air

The air around Earth has not always contained the same mix of gases, and air will continue to change in the future.

A world without air

When the Earth was formed about 4.5 billion years ago, there was probably no atmosphere around it. Volcanoes erupted and a lot of gas was pumped from the ground. Water vapour was also released, and this collected to form the first seas and lakes. Many gases dissolved in the water, leaving behind nitrogen, carbon dioxide and the noble gases. This early atmosphere could not support animal life.

Early plant life

There was very little oxygen in the early atmosphere. We know this because iron laid down in rocks 3 billion years ago shows no sign of rust (rust forms when iron mixes with oxygen and water). Plant life, which began at this time, introduced oxygen into the atmosphere.

▼ *In 1980 the eruption of Mount St Helens, Washington, USA sent huge amounts of dust and ash into the atmosphere.*

▲ *Simple plants, like these algae floating on a pond, were some of the first forms of life.*

The first animals

As plants developed and spread through the oceans and eventually on to the land, they took in carbon dioxide and released more and more oxygen. After another 2 billion years, the first animals developed, with a need to breathe oxygen.

Eruption!

From the beginnings of the Earth to the present day, volcanoes have continued to throw out ash and gas. The eruption at Krakatau in 1883 sent clouds of dust into the air which travelled for ten days before landing 5300 kilometres away.

The clouds of dust and ash from volcanoes block out the Sun and can change the climate. Many scientists think a huge volcanic eruption was

The ice covering Antarctica and the Arctic is several kilometres thick. This has formed from layer upon layer of snow, falling over hundreds of thousands of years. The ice contains atmospheric gases and dust. Scientists have drilled straight down and taken out cylinders, called **ice cores**, from depths of up to 3000 metres. The further down they drill, the older the ice. By analysing the ice, scientists have been able to trace changes in the air dating back more than 100 000 years.

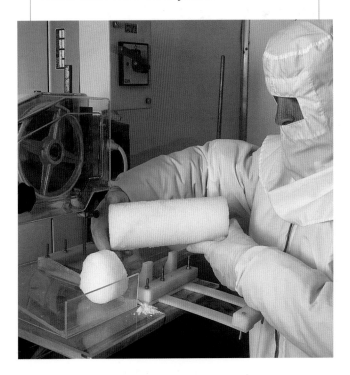

responsible for wiping out all the dinosaurs 65 million years ago. The dust cloud may have blocked out the Sun for several years. In the resulting cold weather plants hardly grew, so the giant reptiles could find no food and eventually died.

Studying air

For the last 400 years people have been devising ways to study air. They have recorded its movement, temperature, pressure and mix of gases.

▲ *Weather vanes placed on tall buildings are a simple but effective way of showing the direction of moving air.*

Early studies of air

In 1593 the Italian scientist Galileo invented the thermometer to record the temperature of the air. This was the first instrument for studying air. Later, in 1643, another Italian called Torricelli developed a barometer to measure the weight of air pressing down on us. In the 1770s oxygen and nitrogen were discovered, followed by the noble gases at the end of the nineteenth century.

Measuring air

One of the oldest devices for measuring air is the weather vane, which is held vertically on a central pivot. One end is broad and catches

▼ *The Beaufort scale is used to describe different wind strengths from 1 to 12, with complete calm registering as 0.*

the wind, bringing the point on the other end round to indicate where the wind is blowing from.

Balloons filled with hydrogen or helium, gases which on their own are lighter than air, carry instruments that measure air temperature, pressure and humidity. Every day 1600 weather balloons are launched around the world, each carrying a **radiosonde** to transmit information to observation stations on the ground. At 27 000 metres the gas inside has expanded so much in the thinner air that the balloons burst, and parachutes take the radiosondes safely down to be used again.

1 light air	2 light breeze	3 gentle breeze	4 moderate breeze	5 fresh breeze	6 strong breeze
1–5 km/h	6–11 km/h	12–19 km/h	20–29 km/h	30–39 km/h	40–50 km/h

▲ *A weather balloon being launched. The balloon will rise to the stratosphere, carrying instruments that measure the air.*

Radar and air masses

Everyday weather is caused by the movement of air masses. These masses take on the temperature of the land or sea underneath. When warm and cold masses meet, the cold mass slides under, forcing the warm mass up. As the warm air rises it can hold less water, and the spare water falls as rain. Observation stations use **radar** to track the movement of air masses and rain clouds.

A network of **satellites** rings the Earth, sending down information about the air. Geo-synchronous satellites remain over the same place, photographing the moving air masses and clouds below. Sun-synchronous satellites circle the Earth, measuring temperature, pressure, and amounts of gases and chemicals.

▼ *This satellite image shows clear skies over most of Europe and a storm over the UK.*

7 high wind
51–61 km/h

8 gale
62–74 km/h

9 strong gale
75–87 km/h

10 storm
89–101 km/h

11 violent storm
102–117 km/h

12 hurricane
more than 118 km/h

Dirty air

Air becomes polluted by gases from cars, factories and open fires. Breathing polluted air can be very harmful.

Exhaust fumes

The engines in cars, buses and lorries emit smoke, which is made up of gases and fine dust particles. Most of the **carbon monoxide** in the air comes from road transport. This gas is absorbed into the blood and makes us feel tired. Other gases, such as sulphur dioxide and nitrogen oxides, worsen breathing illnesses such as asthma. The black smoke from diesel engines in lorries and buses contains fine sooty particles, or hydrocarbons, which can bring cancer-producing chemicals into the body.

▲ *In cities, many cyclists wear masks so that they do not have to breathe in all the pollution from heavy traffic.*

When the smoke clears

When coal was the main heating fuel in houses, millions of chimneys added smoke to city air. In 1952 **smog** killed 3000 people in London. Then in 1955 and again in 1962, hundreds of New Yorkers died as a result of heavy smog. Laws that stopped people burning coal cleaned the air. Today, because of cars, cities such as London, Paris, Athens, Tokyo and Mexico City are suffering from air **pollution** again. New laws are needed to prevent today's smogs.

Stuck in the jam

As cities become overcrowded and there are more and more cars on the roads, the level of gas emissions in the air is higher than ever. When there is no wind, the dirty air collects in the streets, forming smog. In strong sunlight the polluting gases react and produce **ozone**, which causes coughing and choking. In large amounts ozone harms people's lungs and reduces their ability to fight off diseases. In Washington DC, USA, a photo is taken every day to monitor air clarity and quality.

▲ ▼ *Los Angeles bathed in sunlight, with a distant layer of smog trapped against the hills. The picture below shows the city blanketed in smog during a temperature inversion.*

Cars and smog

In many cities smog is a major problem. During the day sunshine heats the ground, which in turn warms the air at ground level. This warm air rises, taking any pollutants with it. But clear nights allow heat to escape, and the ground becomes cold. The ground level air is cooled. Next morning that cool air stays in place. It cannot rise because the air above is warmer and lighter. This is a **temperature inversion**.

In a city such as Los Angeles the gases from five million cars pollute this still air. Often by midday the air has turned to brown smog, which may last for several days, until a change in the weather brings wind or rain to cool the warm air and end the temperature inversion. Now, to stop the smog, tough car emission controls have been introduced.

Spreading pollution

When air pollution is carried by the wind, it can affect people, animals and plants hundreds of kilometres away.

Someone else's smoke

In September 1997 forest fires in Indonesia sent vast clouds of smoke across land hundreds of kilometres away. Thousands of people became ill, schools and businesses closed – and so did airports, after 200 people died in an air crash blamed on the smoke. Despite this experience, not enough was done to stop it from happening again. In 1999 more fires were lit by farmers to clear forests and farmland. Throughout the summer a similar smog settled over Kuala Lumpur in Malaysia. Yellow air hid buildings, made breathing difficult and made people's eyes water.

After the second disaster, South-east Asian governments announced a plan to try to prevent fires, and to educate those who start them. But without new laws, the problem is likely to be repeated every summer.

▼ *Firemen fighting to stop the spread of forest fires in Indonesia.*

▲ *Acid rain and pollution from distant factory chimneys have killed these trees in Wales.*

Acid rain

When sulphur dioxide and nitrogen oxide from road vehicles and power stations mix with water vapour in the air, acid forms. The water vapour may be carried far from the source of pollution. Then it falls as acid rain, damaging trees, killing fish in lakes, harming wildlife and eating away the stonework of buildings. In 1999 the Chinese government reported that acid rain falls on 33 per cent of their country. By the year 2005, half of the UK may be suffering damage from acid rain.

Accident!

As well as the everyday pollution of the air, there is always the risk of industrial accidents that allow poisonous fumes to escape. In 1984 a factory making pesticides in

In 1999, when the number of dead fish floating on the surface of Lake Nyos, Cameroon, increased, local people knew what was happening. Carbon dioxide, bubbling from a volcanic fault beneath the lake, was building up underwater. This had happened before, in 1986, when the carbon dioxide escaped in an explosion. It formed a cloud that drifted over the village, killing 1800 people. Experts rushed to Lake Nyos to prevent a repeat of that tragedy. Pipes were lowered into the 200-metre deep lake to draw out the carbon dioxide safely.

Bophal, India, leaked 5 tonnes of poisonous gas into the air. The lethal cloud spread out and killed 6500 people. Thousands more were injured, many with damaged eyes.

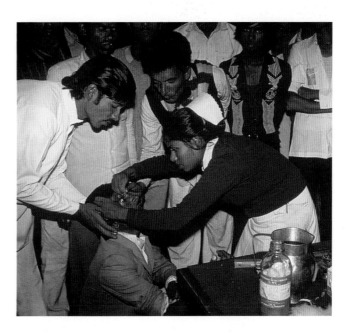

▲ *Nursing victims of the Bhopal disaster.*

Ozone protection

As well as protecting us from meteorites, the atmosphere filters out harmful ultraviolet radiation from the Sun.

The ozone layer

Between 15 and 30 kilometres above our heads, in the stratosphere, lies a layer of gas called ozone. This gas is a type of oxygen that has been altered by sunlight. The ozone layer absorbs 97 per cent of the Sun's ultraviolet radiation. In 1977 the British Antarctic Expedition found a hole in the ozone layer over the South Pole. A decade later the Nimbus 7 satellite recorded a 50 per cent loss of ozone over Antarctica in a month. Sunbathing in nearby Australia suddenly became more dangerous.

Sunburn and skin cancer

A high level of ultraviolet radiation kills off small organisms such as bacteria and viruses. Hospitals and food manufacturers use ultraviolet lamps to sterilize equipment and containers. But radiation can also be harmful because it burns our skin – too much radiation causes skin cancers. Concern about sunbathing dates from the 1970s, when scientists discovered that the ozone layer in the stratosphere was growing thinner.

▼ *This strange bird warns Australians to protect their skin while sunbathing.*

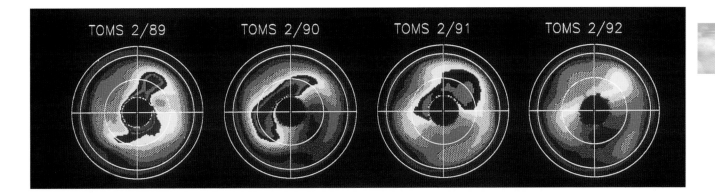

TOMS 2/89   TOMS 2/90   TOMS 2/91   TOMS 2/92

▲ *These satellite images of the North Pole were taken each year from 1989 to 1992. Red shows lots of ozone, green less, yellow very little.*

▼ *These special balloons rise to the top of the stratosphere, where they measure the thickness of the ozone layer.*

CFCs

The gases used in refrigerators, air conditioners, fire extinguishers and some plastics are chemicals called **CFCs (chlorofluorocarbons)**. Once released, these gases stay around for more than 100 years, gradually floating up to the stratosphere. There they are broken down by the Sun and a chemical called chlorine is released, which destroys ozone.

Filling the hole

CFC production rose from 42 000 tonnes in 1950 to 1 250 000 tonnes in 1987 as more aerosols and refrigerators were produced. In 1987, 166 governments met in Montreal, Canada, to sign an agreement: the main industrialized countries agreed to stop producing CFCs within ten years. CFC production fell steeply, but many old refrigerators and plastics continue to release CFCs because the gases are long-lived. The ozone layer will give reduced protection from the Sun for many years and we can expect skin cancers to increase.

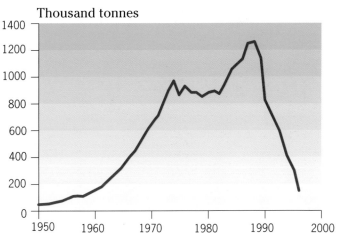

Thousand tonnes

▲ *CFC production fell dramatically after the 1987 agreement.*

Changing climate

Just as the weather changes month by month, so the climate alters through the years. No one is sure why this happens, but several causes have been suggested.

Ice ages

Periods when the world is cold are called ice ages. The earliest known ice age was more than 2 billion years ago, and the most recent began about 50 million years ago. As the climate cooled, glaciers formed in Antarctica until the whole land was covered with ice. Since then there have been periods when the world has warmed up for about 10 000 years, before cooling again – a sequence that has been repeated more than 20 times.

Carbon dioxide and climate

By studying and analysing ice cores, scientists have matched the amount of carbon dioxide (CO_2) in the air with climate. They have found that during the cold of the ice ages, CO_2 levels were low. When the world warmed up, the amount of CO_2 in the air increased by up to 25 per cent. No one yet knows whether that increase caused the climate to become warmer, or was merely the result of it. The only certainty is that more CO_2 in the air is linked to higher world temperatures.

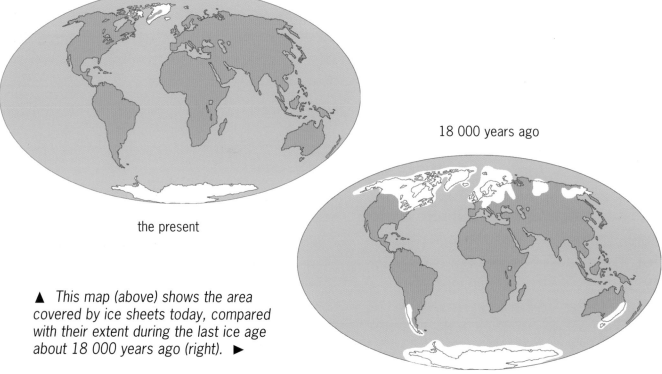

the present

18 000 years ago

▲ *This map (above) shows the area covered by ice sheets today, compared with their extent during the last ice age about 18 000 years ago (right).* ▶

▲ *Glaciers are melting faster than ever as the average world temperature rises.*

A warmer world

Over the last 200 years the industries of the developed world have released more and more **greenhouse gases** into the atmosphere. These gases store some of the Sun's radiation that would otherwise be lost into space, and then give it out as heat.

Carbon dioxide is an important greenhouse gas. Other greenhouse gases are methane from natural gas and farming, nitrous oxide from fertilizers and fires, and CFCs. Over the last century greenhouse gas levels have increased by about 30 per cent, while the average world surface temperature has gone up by almost one degree centigrade.

The effects of global warming are widespread. The sea is rising as the heated water expands and ice melts. Low-lying coasts are being flooded and some islands are in danger of disappearing under the sea. Land far from the oceans is becoming hotter and drier. The climate will continue to become warmer for many years to come, bringing better weather for some, disaster for others.

▲ *In the nineteenth century the chimneys of industrial towns pumped out huge amounts of smoke from burning coal.*

Wood for fires

For thousands of years dead plants, in one form or another, have been a source of fuel for fires. When industry began to grow, the demand for fuel rose – and so did the smoke.

▲ *A fossilized leaf from a seed fern, a tree that grew in forests that were later turned to coal.*

Burning plants

Plants take in carbon dioxide from the air. They release the oxygen but keep the carbon, which makes up 50 per cent of the wood. It is the carbon that burns, giving off carbon dioxide. When humans first learned to make fire, they burned wood from nearby trees to keep warm and to cook food. Half the people on Earth today still use wood for **fuel**. Many areas of open ground have been stripped of wood, so that local people have to travel further and further to find fuel for their needs.

Before the dinosaurs

More than 200 million years ago, before the time of the dinosaurs, plants thrived in the ancient swamps. When they died, they were covered over and gradually squashed. Oxygen and hydrogen from the plants were forced out, leaving the carbon. Today the remains of those ancient plants are mined as coal, which is a **fossil fuel**.

◀ *In a steam engine, burning coal heats water. The steam engine was the main power source for the industrial revolution. Here a steam engine is turning the locomotive's wheels.*

▲ *These Cameroon women spend hours every day collecting firewood.*

Powering industry

With the invention of the steam engine, machines began to take the place of people in industry. The engines used coal to heat water until it turned to steam. Britain was the first industrialized country, making use of its huge coal reserves. Europe and the USA soon followed.

Burning fossils

Petroleum and natural gas were formed under similar conditions to coal and are also fossil fuels. They are the remains of tiny sea creatures and plants that died millions of years ago. At first petroleum, also called crude oil, was made into paraffin, or

More from less

One way of reducing the amount of harmful emissions from fossil fuels is to use these fuels more efficiently. Where oil is found underground, there is often natural gas present. In the past this gas was burnt off. In 1995, 95 per cent of the gas found in the Mexican oilfield was wasted by burning it. In 1997 Mexico, along with most other countries, agreed to lower greenhouse emissions. Now they pipe away and use 98 per cent of the natural gas.

kerosene, and used mainly for lighting and heating. More recently petroleum has been used as a fuel for cars, lorries, ships and aeroplanes. These pump out greenhouse gases.

Power for people

The electricity that drives so many of our household gadgets is generated at power stations. These great energy converters need fuel to fire them. For many years they have burned fossil fuel.

Using coal

Today coal is more popular than ever as a fuel. Over the last 50 years the amount used worldwide has doubled. Most of it is used for generating electricity. In China 75 per cent of electricity is generated by coal-fired power stations. The coal is burned to heat water until it turns into steam. Under pressure, this steam drives turbines that generate electricity. The carbon from the fuel is released into the air as smoke.

Oil-powered stations

Oil now supplies 50 per cent of the world's total energy. As well as providing fuel for aeroplanes and road vehicles, it is used to generate about 20 per cent of the world's electricity. This thick liquid is difficult to transport and causes pollution when it leaks. When it is burned at the power station, it

▲ *These four cooling towers emit only steam, but the chimney is releasing greenhouse gases.*

An endless fuel

Modern sewage treatment plants produce large amounts of sludge that has to be disposed of, either in landfills or as a fertilizer. Now a new use for sewage sludge is being tried out in Japan. A factory converts it into a substitute for coal, called fuel slurry. Burning fuel slurry emits fewer greenhouse gases than burning coal, while disposing of an endless supply of common waste. Now a similar factory is being built in the USA.

releases greenhouse gases into the air. The advantages of oil as a fuel are the fact that it burns easily and gives off a lot of heat.

▲ *Streaks of oil darken the waters around a leaking tanker in Galveston Bay, Texas, USA.*

Gas-powered stations

If oil underground continues to decay, natural gas is produced. This can easily be brought to the surface and transported through pipes. When natural gas burns it gives off fewer greenhouse gases than other fossil fuels. Many countries, among them the UK, USA and China, are now using more natural gas as a fuel in order to reduce the amount of greenhouse gas emissions.

▼ *Oil wells in Kuwait, set alight during the Gulf War, were still burning ten months later in October 1991.*

Cleaner and cheaper

As electricity use increases, so the search continues to find cleaner and cheaper ways of generating it. But there are other pollutants besides dirty smoke.

High hopes

The energy stored in a small lump of a rock called uranium is equivalent to the energy in many tonnes of coal. In a nuclear reactor the energy is released and used to heat water into steam that drives turbines. There are no harmful emissions, and the process is very cheap. Fifty years ago people thought that nuclear power was the energy source of the future, and 25 countries, including the UK, USA and France, began to build nuclear power stations.

▲ *Nuclear power stations have no smoking chimneys, but can be dangerous in other ways.*

Radioactivity

Radiation given out by uranium is harmful. Sudden exposure to high levels of radiation causes diarrhoea, loss of hair, skin burns and death. Several years after even a small dose of radiation, cancers can form and babies can be affected in the womb. About 0.3 per cent of the uranium used in nuclear power stations remains unchanged at the end of the process. This nuclear waste used to be dumped in the sea, but fish and shellfish took in the radiation, so sea dumping was banned. Now waste is sealed deep underground in concrete.

◄ *When the nuclear power station at Chernobyl, Ukraine, exploded in 1986, deadly radiation covered nearby land. This school was abandoned.*

▲ *Protesters demanding the closure of Three Mile Island power station in 1989, ten years after the nuclear accident there.*

In the air

Nuclear power was popular in the USA until 1979, when an accident at the Three Mile Island power plant showed the dangers of radiation. Contaminated water flooded one of the buildings and radioactive gas escaped. Carried on the wind, the gas drifted over local houses, from which 200 000 people fled.

No one can tell how many people will develop cancer because of this accident, but a study has shown that at least 430 children have already died. Their deaths may have resulted from the effects of the radiation. It could have been worse – the reactor almost exploded.

Dream or nightmare?

Despite the proven dangers, nuclear power has not been abandoned. Europe has half the world's nuclear power stations, which provide 35 per cent of Europe's electricity. Although most European countries are unlikely to build more stations, they intend to keep the ones they have. In Asia some countries are still attracted by the dream of cheap power with no greenhouse gas emissions and are building new nuclear stations. Only time will tell whether that dream can be realized safely.

The accident turned people in the USA against nuclear power stations. No new stations have been built, and those that have closed down have not been replaced.

Age-old power

Traditional ways of producing power inspire today's engineers and scientists. Used carefully, these natural sources will keep our air clean.

Power from the Sun

In just half an hour the Earth receives enough energy from the Sun to satisfy all its power needs for a year. To gather that energy, **solar photovoltaic panels** have been developed. These generate electricity when sunlight falls on them. The first solar-powered house in the UK had 48 panels in its roof, generating more than enough electricity to run computers, a washing machine and televisions. In Chicago, USA, disused factories are being fitted with solar panels to provide electricity for nearby offices and homes.

A wide range of fuels

The range of fuels used to generate electricity in the future could be very wide. In Sri Lanka a local firm is building a generator powered by charcoal waste. In Australia, sawdust from timber works will become a fuel in a specially-designed power station. And in the USA a new process will turn sewage into a fuel to replace coal, generating less carbon dioxide and using a raw material that will never be in short supply.

▼ *Solar power plants like this one in Italy produce electricity without creating pollution.*

▲ *Wind farms are built on high ground or by the sea, where the wind is strong and constant. This wind farm is in the mountains of California, USA.*

Moving air

Windmills were once a common form of power generator, turning mill wheels and pumping water before electricity was discovered. Today more and more wind turbines are being used to produce electricity. Wind farms consist of groups of giant wind turbines scattered over a large area. They are sited in windy places away from towns, but some people object to the way they look, and they can be noisy. The advantage of wind turbines is that they generate clean electricity. Now wind farms are being built out at sea.

In Toronto, Canada, two windmills are being built in the city centre. Local people will be able to choose whether they buy electricity from there, or from cheaper – but dirtier – fossil fuel generators.

▶ *Water flowing through the Glen Canyon Dam, USA, turns turbines to generate cheap, clean electricity.*

Going with the flow

For centuries watermills have used the movement of water as it flows downhill to provide power. Today that same process generates 25 per cent of the world's electricity. Dams are built across river valleys to create huge reservoirs of water. This water flows down past electricity generating turbines. No pollution is released into the air, but the valleys that have been flooded with water are changed dramatically.

Hydroelectric power stations produce 63 per cent of Vietnam's electricity. With demand for electricity rising, Vietnam is planning a new scheme that will be three times the size of the present largest station. To make way for the new dam and the flooding that will follow, more than 100 000 people will be moved into new houses. As most are farmers, they will also need new jobs.

Natural power sources

In the future much of our power may be generated by making use of natural sources, which have been around for billions of years.

The moving sea

Anyone who has watched the tide come in or been to the coast on a windy day will know the power of the sea. Tides can turn turbines under water. France has built a tidal **barrage** at La Rance to harness this power. Tidal barrages may harm coastal wildlife, so using waves might be better. Platforms or ships would work out at sea, using the movement of waves to turn turbines.

▲ *In Thailand small biogas tanks produce fuel from local waste. They are cheap to use and easy to maintain.*

▼ *This landfill site in Chicago, USA, is covered with a giant plastic sheet to keep in methane gas. The gas can later be used for fuel.*

In hot water

In some parts of the Earth, such as Iceland and Rotorua in New Zealand, the rocks close to the surface are very hot and water held underground gushes out steaming. Steam can be used to generate electricity. In the USA geothermal power stations generate as much electricity as three nuclear power stations.

Geothermal systems drill down to hot rock, which lies between 300 and 3000 metres below the surface. Water is pumped down to be heated and turned into steam, and is then used to generate electricity. Geothermal power could provide half of all the electricity needed without harming the environment where the geology is right, such as in Africa, and Central and South America.

Fuel from waste

Cow dung and rotting waste produce a gas called methane, which can be used as a fuel. Called biogas, it can be collected and burnt. In Almora, India, the people have been given biogas cookers that burn gas produced by local herds of cows. Now there is no need for them to destroy trees for firewood. In the West, sewage works and landfill sites both produce methane as a fuel. There are more than 70 biogas sites in the USA. The largest, at Puente Hills, California, powers a 46 megawatt

Biomass fuels

Anything natural that can be burned to produce heat that generates electricity is called biomass. Grass, trees and the leftovers of farmed crops are all potential biomass fuels. The state of Iowa, USA, is planning to farm switch grass, willows and poplars for fuel. In the UK, willow biomass (below) will be used to fuel a major power station in Yorkshire.

electricity generator. Burning coal to make that much power would release 290 000 tonnes of carbon dioxide.

A huge store of methane lies frozen under the oceans. Japanese scientists are trying to extract this methane, which could supply the world's energy needs for the next 200 years.

New inventions

Governments are reducing greenhouse gas emissions and developing less polluting technology. Many private companies are also working towards a cleaner environment.

Electric cars

Cars powered by electricity move without sending out smoke, but the batteries needed to store the power are heavy. Until now electric cars have been slow and unable to travel more than about 100 kilometres before their batteries need to be recharged. A new generation of cars could change all that. Manufacturers such as Twike of Switzerland have produced an improved battery that charges more quickly and gives the car a greater travelling distance. The electric car is recharged by plugging it into a power point. This reduces pollution because power stations – particularly those using natural sources – are relatively clean compared with cars.

▼ *A prototype fuel cell car, made in Europe, which runs without releasing any pollution.*

▲ *A man fills his pick-up with hydrogen at a refuelling station in Los Angeles, USA.*

The fuel cell

In 1839 a fuel cell was developed that works by forcing hydrogen and oxygen to join together, producing water and an electrical current that can be used to power a motor. Apart from a little heat, there are no emissions. The problem with the fuel cell was the high cost, but Mercedes-Benz hope to produce the first reasonably-priced hydrogen powered vehicle by the year 2005.

In Europe a fuel cell has been developed that runs on natural gas, but new technology means that carbon dioxide emissions can be removed. An electricity generating station consisting of hundreds of fuel cells would be virtually free from dangerous greenhouse gas emissions.

Super cars

Developments in engine technology have made cars more efficient, so that they need less fuel. But today's cars will seem wasteful beside the next generation. The Nissan Sentra produces fewer emissions on a 30-km drive than an ordinary car parked with its engine running.

A new motor

Petrol engines consist of hundreds of moving parts, each of which does a different job. This makes them relatively inefficient, and they use a large amount of fuel. For many years engineers have tried, without success, to develop better engines. Now an Australian engineer has produced the OX2 motor, which has only three moving parts. Compared with a normal engine the OX2 is easy to maintain, uses less fuel, is more powerful, and has lower emissions.

▲ *This car, with its plastic body, can be completely recycled.*

How you can help

Factories can cut air pollution by pumping out less dirt and gases. Car manufacturers can make vehicles that run efficiently. All of us can help save energy and improve the quality of the air.

Switching off

Using less energy at home is easy – turning off lights that are not needed reduces not only the electricity bill but also air pollution at the power station. Leaving a television on stand-by instead of switching off the power may not seem wasteful, but many machines on stand-by use as much as 80 per cent of the electricity they use when they are working. If everyone living in the UK switched off their televisions, video recorders and computers instead of leaving them on stand-by, half a million tonnes of greenhouse gases, pumped out by power stations, could be saved every year.

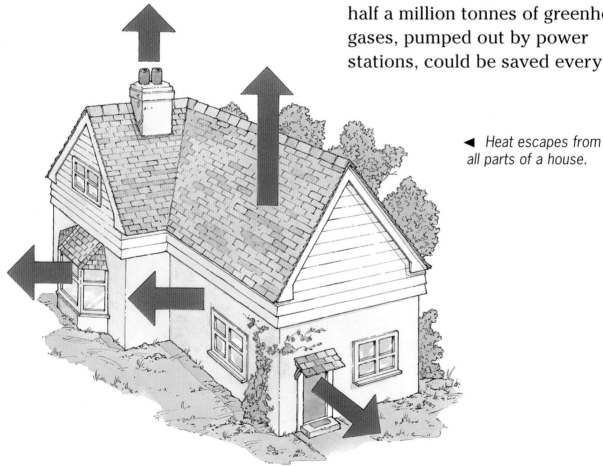

◄ *Heat escapes from all parts of a house.*

Looking after itself

In the future more houses may be able to generate their own power, collect their own water and process their own sewage. This is how a new house in Wales works. The house has solar panels and a wind turbine to generate electricity. South-facing walls are made of glass to catch the sun, while efficient insulation means that little heat is lost through the walls and roof. Rainwater is piped to a store in the basement, which provides the water supply. The house was 25 per cent more expensive to build than an ordinary house because of its environmentally-friendly features, but the owners know they are helping to conserve energy and will not be responsible for polluting the air.

▲ *Most towns have bins where people can leave their newspapers and bottles to be sorted and recycled.*

▲ *This house in Wales takes its electricity from solar panels. To generate the same amount of electricity, a coal power station would release 2½ tonnes of carbon dioxide every year.*

Less packaging

If we produce less waste, such as rubbish from packaging, we save in two ways. Sweet wrappers and plastic bags are made using energy, and have to be disposed of using energy. Both processes produce pollution. We can help by saying 'no' to packaging.

Plant a tree

By planting a tree, you help to improve air quality. Trees take in carbon dioxide, the main greenhouse gas, and give out the oxygen that we need to breathe. Choose a species that grows naturally in your area, because a native tree will attract and support the local wildlife. Saplings about 1 metre high are cheap to buy and easy to grow.

Air projects

Here are three fun ways to find out about air and what it can do.

Heavy air

Air is invisible, yet it keeps us on the ground. This experiment proves that air is heavy stuff!

You will need two balloons, some string and a stick. Blow up the balloons and tie them to either end of a stick. Now tie a string to the centre of the stick. Hold the string so that the stick and the balloons balance. The weight of the two balloons with air inside them is equal.

Now pop one of the balloons and see what happens. Without the air inside it, the burst balloon is lighter, so that end of the stick rises.

The lichen test

Any exposed stone or tree trunk can provide a home for lichens. These strange organisms consist of a partnership of a fungus, which forms the main body, and an alga. Lichens provide a good test for air pollution because they are sensitive to sulphur dioxide.

Look around your local area for lichens. They take a long time to grow, so look at older stones and buildings. Gravestones in a cemetery are a good place to start. Make a note of where you find lichen, and its type. Leafy lichens, which look like tiny forests, will only grow in clean air. Flat lichens do not mind some air pollution. If you find no lichen at all, that may be because you live in an area where the air is heavily polluted with sulphur dioxide.

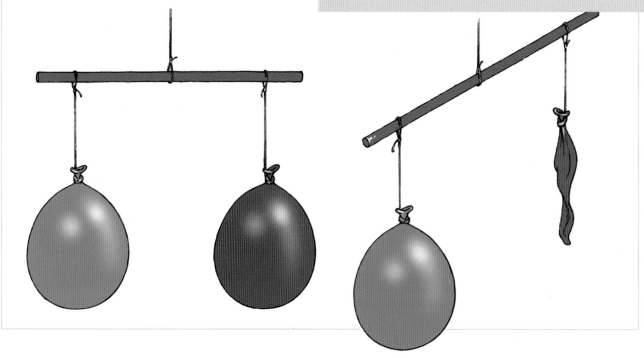

A paper plane

You probably know how to make a paper dart that shoots through the air when you throw it. Here's how to make a plane that flies just like the real thing.

1. Take a square sheet of paper and fold over one edge. Fold that edge again, rolling up the paper and flattening it until you reach about halfway across.

2. Fold the paper in half along its length and cut out the shape of a front wing and a smaller rear wing, as shown.

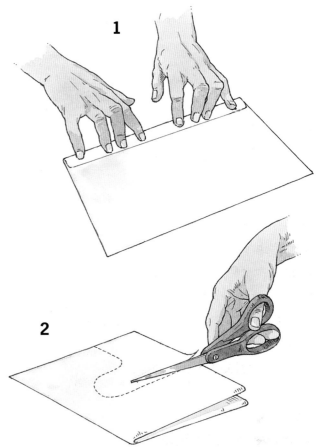

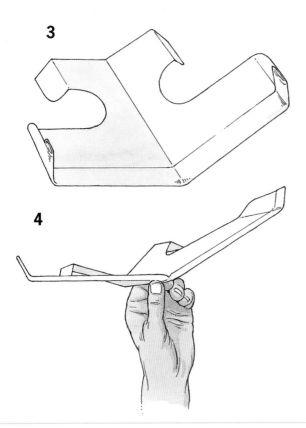

3. Open out and fold up the ends of the wings. Fold down the rear wings.

4. Hold the front edge between your thumb and first finger and push forward gently to launch the plane.

By folding the rear edges of the wings up or down, you can make flaps that will alter the direction of flight, just like a real plane.

Air facts and figures

As light as air

The total weight of all the air around Earth is approximately 5 200 000 000 000 000 tonnes.

At sea level one cubic metre of air, which is the amount contained in a large cardboard box such as a washing machine is delivered in, weighs 1.17 kilograms.

Although winds of over 100 km/h are rare at surface level, higher in the atmosphere air moves much faster. Bands of wind about 10-15 kilometres up are called jet streams. A jet stream can blow at over 320 km/h. Jet streams are only a few hundred kilometres wide, but may stretch halfway round the Earth.

Race with the Sun

The Third World Solar Cycle Challenge, held in Australia in 1999, lasted for seven days and covered 1 500 kilometres. This cycle (left), which travels at about 50 km/h, was made by students from Southampton University, England. Half the power comes from solar panels on the body, the rest from pedals turned by the rider. One of the dangers faced by the riders is that animals and birds on the empty Australian roads do not jump out of the way for these silent, clean machines.

Air pollution

The amount of carbon dioxide in the air of the troposphere has risen from 288 parts per million (ppm) in 1860 to 364 ppm today. Methane has increased from 848 to 1800 ppm and nitrous oxide is up from 285 ppm to 312 ppm. These increases have been caused by emissions from factories, power stations and vehicles. The town with the world's worst air pollution is Dzerzhinsk in Russia, where 600 tonnes of poisonous gas is released from chimneys each year.

Billions of aerosols

Polluted air carries a greater load of aerosols, which cling to the pollutants. One cubic metre of clean air over the ocean contains about one billion aerosol particles. In a city the dirty air may contain 100 billion aerosol particles.

How far up?

The atmosphere stretches up for 1000 kilometres from the surface of planet Earth. This is not as far as it may sound. If you could drive a car straight up at 50 km/h, you would be in space in less than a day. You could walk to the top of troposphere, a distance of 15 kilometres, in just a few hours. We live in a thin layer called the biosphere, between the ground and the point where the air becomes too thin to breathe.

Worst smog

The city with the worst smog in the world is Mexico City, where ozone levels in the smog caused by vehicles and factories sometimes rises to over 200 parts per billion (ppb). Other cities are not far behind.

Los Angeles has for many years been the US city with the worst smog. In 1999 ozone levels rose above the federal safe limit of 125 ppb on 43 days, reaching 170 ppb on one occasion.

Now Los Angeles has a rival. The air in Houston, the USA's fourth largest city, is becoming dirtier and dirtier. Some days the ozone level touches 200 ppb, as high as in Mexico City. In 1999 it overtook Los Angeles and became the USA's number one smog city.

Air and energy worldwide

By looking at these maps you can compare areas where energy resources are found with areas where they are used. Fossil fuels are still the world's great energy source, and the cause of much of its air pollution.

Areas that use more energy are those which have most energy resources. This is because transporting coal and natural gas is expensive. Burning fossil fuels, especially coal, produces acid rain. Winds carry the pollution, so some producers do not suffer as much as the countries downwind of them. Some parts of the world, such as South America, appear to have few energy resources. In fact, it may have a wealth of untapped resources, but reaching them would harm the environment.

Energy resources around the world

▼ *The world's energy resources are constantly changing as new fossil fuel fields are found underground, and nuclear and hydroelectric power stations are built or demolished.*

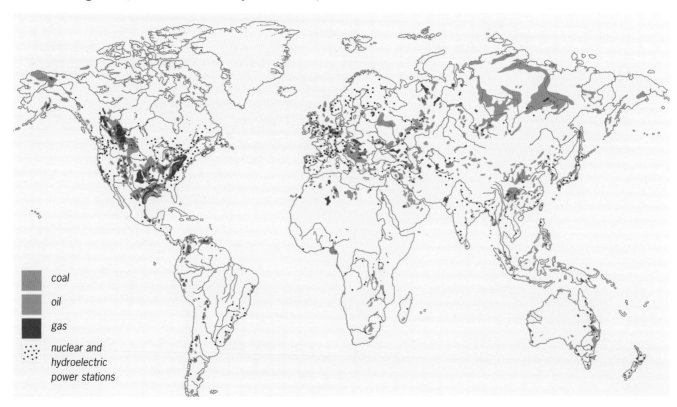

coal

oil

gas

nuclear and hydroelectric power stations

Acid rain around the world

▼ *Acid rain is measured on a pH scale: pH 7.0 is neutral, with no acid; pH 5.0 is slightly acid and pH 4.0 or less is very acid.*

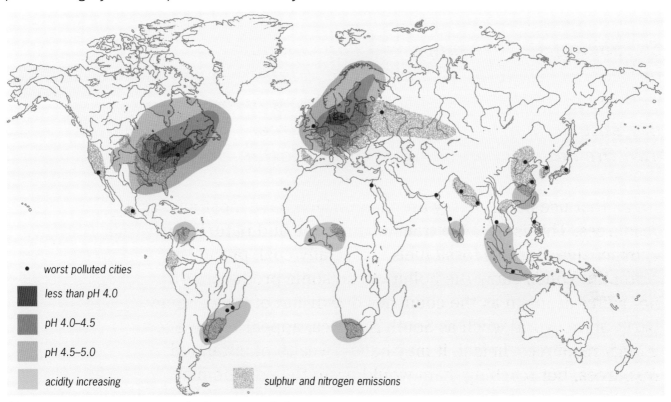

- • worst polluted cities
- less than pH 4.0
- pH 4.0–4.5
- pH 4.5–5.0
- acidity increasing
- sulphur and nitrogen emissions

Energy use around the world

▼ *Different parts of the world use vastly different amounts of energy. People in Europe and the USA consume more energy in a day than those in Central Africa use in a week.*

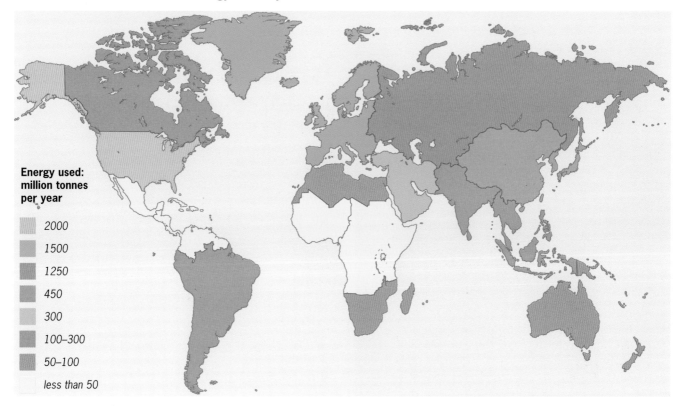

Energy used: million tonnes per year

- 2000
- 1500
- 1250
- 450
- 300
- 100–300
- 50–100
- less than 50

Further information

Air is a resource we should all have a say in. A few people talking about clean air may not be heard, but a lot of people together can make a difference. The following groups work to conserve and improve the environment.

The Centre for Alternative Technology

is based at a former quarry in Wales, where a group of people try out new equipment. CAT produces books and leaflets for young people, and the visitor complex welcomes families and school parties. There are energy displays, examples of practical solutions using windmills and solar power, friendly animals, an adventure playground and a restaurant.
Machynlleth, Powys SY20 9AZ
http://www.cat.org.uk

The Council for Environmental Education

is the national body for environmental education, providing information on teaching resources.
University of Reading, London Road,
Reading RG1 5AQ
http://www.cee.org.uk

The Earth Centre is a visitor centre that gives advice on sustainable living and how we can be more environmentally friendly.
Denaby Main, Conisborough, Doncaster,
South Yorkshire, DN12 4EA

The Environment Agency is the government information service for England and Wales. It supplies news, information and facts about current environmental problems and issues, and can provide posters and worksheets for young people.
Rio House, Waterside Drive, Aztec West,
Almondsbury, Bristol BS12 4UD
http://www.environment-agency.gov.uk

◄ *These local people in Scotland have got together to plant trees that will transform their environment.*

Friends of the Earth (FoE) is the largest network of environmental groups in the world. They provide free leaflets and Youth Campaign packs, which contain information and ideas for protecting the conditions for life on Earth. 26-28 Underwood Street, London N1 7JQ. http://www.foe.co.uk

Greenpeace campaigns against air pollution, and promotes clean energy sources. Canonbury Villas, London N1 2PN. http://www.greenpeace.org.uk/greenbytes

The Meteorological Office looks at all aspects of the weather, including climate change and the ozone layer. It publishes free leaflets, teaching packs, videos and books. The Enquiries Office, London Road, Bracknell, Berkshire RG12 2SZ. http://www.meto.gov.uk

▼ *These clean air demonstrators in Budapest wear masks to emphasize their message.*

Further reading

Keeping the Air Clean by John Baines (Wayland, 1997)

Atlas of Endangered Resources by Steve Pollock (Belitha Press, 1995)

New Technology: Energy by Nigel Hawkes (Gloucester Press, 1994)

Air Pollution (Friends of the Earth, 1994)

Energy (Friends of the Earth, 1993)

The Ozone Layer by M Bright (Gloucester Press, 1991)

Air and Oceans by Dougal Dixon (Wayland, 1990)

Exploring Energy Sources by Ed Catherall (Wayland, 1990)

The Climate Crisis by John Becklake (Watts, 1989)

National Society for Clean Air and Environmental Protection (NSCA)

works to protect the environment by reducing air pollution and noise. 136 North Street, Brighton BN1 1RG. http://www.greenchannel.com/nsca

Wildlife Trusts look after areas where wild plants and animals are allowed to thrive. You can help with the work of clearing up these sites and plant new trees. They run Wildlife Watch, an environmental club that involves children and young people in practical projects such as monitoring acid rain, water pollution and smog. Leaflets, posters and educational packs are available. The Kiln, Waterside, Mather Road, Newark, Nottinghamshire NG24 1WT. http://www.wildlifetrust.org.uk

Glossary

aerosols Particles of dust, sand and microbes carried in the air.

air The mix of gases around the Earth.

aqualung A bottle of air that allows divers to breath underwater.

argon A gas without smell or colour found in the atmosphere.

atmosphere The gases surrounding Earth, mostly nitrogen (78%) and oxygen (21%).

bacteria Tiny living things that help to break down dead plants and animals.

barrage A construction that forms a barrier in a river.

carbon dioxide A gas that makes up about 0.4 per cent of the air, but is increasing. It is the main greenhouse gas.

carbon monoxide A poisonous gas without colour or smell, produced when carbon burns in a place where there is little air.

CFCs (chlorofluorocarbons) Mixtures of the chemicals chlorine, fluorine and carbon used in industry and in refrigerators. They are long-lasting, but when released into the air they gradually rise to the stratosphere, where they decay in sunlight. This produces chlorine, which removes ozone from the air.

compressed air Air squeezed into a container, such as a tyre or a bottle.

condense To turn from vapour to liquid.

eco-system A community of living things of various species.

evaporation The changing of a liquid into a vapour or gas.

exosphere The top layer of the atmosphere.

fossil fuel Fuels, including coal, gas and oil, formed millions of years ago from the remains of plants.

fuel Anything that gives off energy or heat when burnt.

greenhouse gases Gases in the air that store heat from the Sun that would otherwise be lost in space. The more of these gases in the air, the greater the amount of heat is stored.

helium A gas in the air that is very light.

humidity The amount of water in the air.

ice core A sample of ice taken by drilling through a layer of ice.

insulator Anything that stops heat moving. An insulator around a hot-water tank stops the heat escaping.

krypton A noble gas found in small amounts in the air, used in light bulbs.

mesosphere The layer of Earth's atmosphere above the stratosphere, where the air is thin and temperatures low.

microbes Tiny organisms that can only be seen through a microscope.

neon A noble gas found in the air, used to fill orange streetlights.

nitrogen The most plentiful gas in the air.

noble gases Those gases in the air, such as neon and krypton, that until recently were thought to be unable to mix or react with other gases and chemicals.

oxygen A gas in the air that all life needs to survive. We take it in when we breathe.

ozone A form of oxygen that is poisonous and formed by sunlight on smog. In the stratosphere ozone absorbs the Sun's harmful radiation.

particles The tiny pieces left when any material breaks up or is eroded.

photosynthesis The process by which plants use sunlight and water to convert carbon dioxide into food.

pollution Damage to any part of the environment, such as air, water or land.

radar A machine that finds and locates objects in the air over great distances.

radiation A form of energy given off by radioactive material.

radiosonde A machine that sends radio signals.

satellites Spacecraft that circle, or orbit, a planet. Geo-synchronous satellites circle Earth at the same speed as the planet's spin, enabling them to stay over one place. Sun-synchronous satellites circle round and round the planet, passing bit by bit above every part of the surface.

smog A harmful mixture of fog and exhaust gases, such as those from cars, fires and factories.

solar photovoltaic panels Special sheets that convert sunlight into electricity.

stratosphere The second layer of the atmosphere around Earth, above the troposphere and below the mesosphere.

temperature inversion A layer of cool air at ground level, trapped under a layer of warm air.

thermosphere A layer of atmosphere around Earth that extends for about 600 kilometres above the mesosphere.

troposphere The lowest layer of the atmosphere, resting on the Earth's surface.

water vapour The gas that water turns into when it evaporates, for example steam.

xenon A noble gas found in the atmosphere.

Index